DOCKSIDE

STAGE
4
BOOK 7

CRAZIEST CROOKS

Sue Graves

RISING STARS

It was a hot day. Roo and Lee were playing basketball.

"I'm better than you," said Lee,
as she shot the ball into the hoop.

Roo got the ball and spun it higher into the air. It shot into the hoop. "Look!" he said. "I'm much better than you."

Later, it got even hotter. Roo and Lee sat in the shade, closer to the bins where it was cooler. They spotted a van.

"That's the rustiest, dirtiest van I've ever seen!" said Roo. "What's it doing here?" asked Lee.

Two men got out and put up a ladder at the back of the flats.

"They must be window cleaners," said Lee. "They must be the *craziest* window cleaners then," said Roo. "They don't have any water or cleaning stuff."

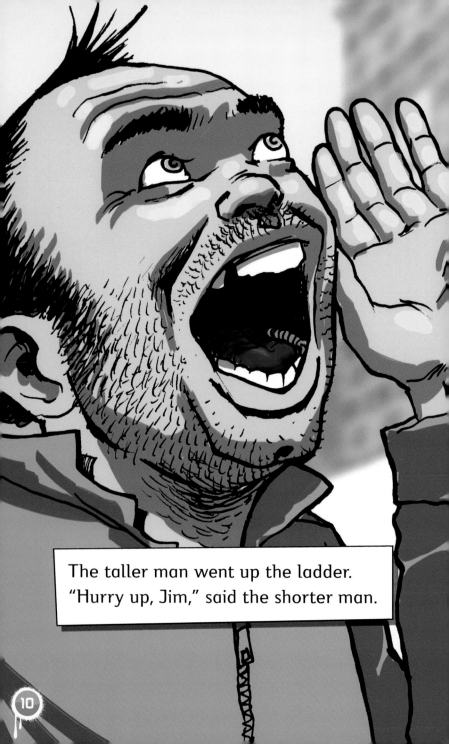

The taller man went up the ladder.
"Hurry up, Jim," said the shorter man.

"Shut up, Andy!" said Jim. "It's harder to hurry when it's hot like this."

Jim pushed open a window. Then Andy went up the ladder. The men climbed through the window.

"Oh no!" said Lee. "They're breaking into one of the flats. What shall we do?"

"Call the police of course," said Roo.

Suddenly, Roo saw the men climbing back out of the window.

"They're stealing a TV," Roo said. "We'll soon see about that! I've got a plan."

Roo ran and grabbed the ladder. He pulled it away from the wall.

"Oi, kid!" shouted Jim. "Bring that back."

The men got crosser and crosser.
They got madder and madder.
Then Andy fell. He grabbed at Jim.

"Help!" he screamed. "I'm slipping."